THE BRITISH MUSEUM

CLASSICAL
LOVE POETRY

THE BRITISH MUSEUM
CLASSICAL
LOVE POETRY

Edited and translated by
Jonathan Williams and Clive Cheesman

THE BRITISH MUSEUM PRESS

Deliciis suis peregrinis uterque

© 2004, 2013 The Trustees of The British Museum

Jonathan Williams and Clive Cheesman have asserted the right to be identified as the authors of this work

First published in 2004 by The British Museum Press
A division of The British Museum Company Ltd
38 Russell Square, London WC1B 3QQ
britishmuseum.org/publishing

This edition published 2013

ISBN 978 0 7141 2280 9

Designed by Caroline and Roger Hillier
The Old Chapel Graphic Design
www.theoldchapelivinghoe.com

Printed in China by 1010 Printing Co.

Papers used by the British Museum Press are recyclable products made from wood grown in well-managed forests and other controlled sources. The manufacturing processes conform to the environmental regulations of the country of origin.

Page 1 Black-glazed drinking vessel with seated hunter (detail – *see* p. 49). Pottery, Etruscan, *c.*300–280 BC. Diam. 17.8 cm. British Museum 1855,0306.16, donated by Chambers Hall.

Frontispiece Edward Burne Jones, *Love in a Tangle* (detail – *see* p. 59). Watercolour. English, AD 1882–98. Diam. 16.2 cm. British Museum 1909,0512.1.15.

The majority of artworks illustrated in this book are from the collection of the British Museum – *see* page 96.

CONTENTS

INTRODUCTION

'Cherishing Venus, delight of gods and men . . .'

With this impassioned invocation of the Roman goddess of love, Lucretius began one of the most extraordinary poems of Classical antiquity, *On the Nature of the Universe* (*see* p. 56). The rest of the poem's 5,000 lines consist of a detailed account of Epicurean philosophical theory. Not, on the face of it, a sexy subject. But its opening passage is one of the most intense evocations of love in Greek and Roman literature. In Lucretius' hands Venus becomes the primal generative energy behind all things, surging powerfully throughout creation. Everything lies under her tender might.

Here we meet a rather different notion of the ancient gods of love from that conveyed, for instance, by the famous statue of Eros in London's Piccadilly Circus where Love is a harmless child, innocently, if playfully, shooting arrows into the human heart. The love gods that so fascinated the poets of Greece and Rome invaded the mind, took possession of the body, distracted the senses, and goaded the heart into sexual obsession and physical madness. They were an irresistible force of nature, as destructive as they were delightful.

Hesiod, the earliest poet of ancient Greece whose name is known to us, characterized Eros as one of the first deities to be born, alongside other elemental gods such as Chaos and Night. Long before Zeus and Athena there was Love, creating the universe and 'loosening limbs' – no sentimentalized Cupid he.

Francesco Xanto Avelli da Rovigo (attrib.), front of plate from a birth set, *Venus and Cupids in Vulcan's Forge* (detail). Maiolica. From Urbino, Italy, AD 1539. Diam. 17.1 cm. British Museum 1878,1230.373, bequeathed by John Henderson.

Where did this ancient vision of the divine power of Love come from? Why is it so different from later versions? Christianity changed perceptions, of course, at least in the West. In Christian tradition human love acquired exalted connotations of sacrifice, duty and purity which, to some extent, still linger today. The language of passion and desire was consigned to the world of sin, except paradoxically when applied to the human soul's deep longing for God. The influence of Christianity may now be waning, but other modern ideas – such as romance – continue to blur our understanding of Greek and Roman love.

But if we do now feel less uncomfortable with the intensely sexual nature of much ancient love poetry than, say, our nineteenth-century predecessors, this isn't because our moral universe has become more aligned with that of antiquity. We live in a world where sexual morality is governed by a largely *laissez-faire* ethos. Anything goes, so long as it's consenting and nobody gets hurt. Social relations between men and women, too, are liberal and open, at least in theory.

Attitudes could not have been more different in Greece and Rome. Eros acquired his reputation as a violent agitator in a world where relations between the sexes and across different sectors of society were highly regulated. Men and women grew up apart and were socialized separately. Association across the gender barrier was tightly chaperoned by families, especially among social elites of the kind to which the poets of antiquity belonged. In such an atmosphere, where free access to the opposite sex was restricted, the merest glimpse of a woman's ankle was enough to send a young man into paroxysms of desire, and vice versa. It also induced a strong tendency towards homoeroticism.

How did people cope with Eros's onslaught under these circumstances? Marriage was one obvious way out, though partners were probably seldom chosen freely. Strong passions, if illicitly consummated, could lead to personal tragedy or social death.

Prostitutes were available, and not necessarily the disrespectable option, for those who could afford them.

Upper-class Greeks and Romans lived lives circumscribed by social convention. Contrary to the headlong, full-on decadent lifestyle of modern imagination, it was probably rather straight-laced by our standards. As is often the case in such societies, people used imaginative literature or art to express their playful fantasies. And not surprisingly, they did this rather more frequently than writing about the humdrum world of daily experience. Ancient poetry liked to play with the rules, and sometimes ignore them altogether. But it also probably had the effect on the ancient reader of highlighting, and often reconfirming, the boundaries according to which they lived. Our mistake has often been to confuse ancient fiction with ancient reality.

This volume collects together an anthology of translated Greek and Latin love poetry, including some famous pieces and, we hope, some less well-known offerings, covering 2,000 years, from the eighth century BC to the early Middle Ages. We had to begin with the poet, or poetic tradition, known to the Greeks as Homer, whose two great epics the *Iliad* and the *Odyssey* were fundamental texts for the Greek-speaking world from the eighth century BC right down to medieval Byzantium. What makes Homer stand out in the passage chosen for this selection is his focus on the importance of domestic love (*see* p. 88). The portrayal of Hector and Andromache represents a deeply attractive ideal of enduring faithfulness and familial affection. They clearly love each other, and we cannot but sympathize with their emotions as they take their leave from one another, uncertain whether this will be the last time or not. The kind of love we encounter here is the glue that keeps two individuals together through difficult times.

Things look rather different in the world of the Greek lyric poets of the seventh to fifth centuries BC – represented here by selections from Sappho, Ibycus, Anacreon and Pindar. They invented Love as the maddening gadfly whose sting pierces body and mind. This is no game: his wounds can kill. The passionate intensity expressed in these early poems is in many ways unsurpassed in later Greek literature. Nevertheless, it is this sense of the irresistible, physical force exerted by Love that distinguishes these poems from many of their successors in later centuries whose aesthetic was often rather more light-hearted and self-consciously witty. Contrast, for instance, the image of Love as a boxer (a brutal sport in ancient Greece, it is worth remembering, involving knuckle-dusters and lots of blood) in one of the poems of Anacreon selected here (*see* p. 32), with the delightful scenario presented in a poem after the style of Anacreon, but probably written much later, in which Love, posing as a little boy lost, tricks his way into the author's house and heart at the dead of night (see p. 36).

So where was all this passion heading, what was it meant to lead to? What of lifelong love, love matches and marriage for love? Marriage and monogamy were institutions held up for admiration as much by the Greeks and Romans as by any that have come after them. Homer, as we have seen, provided the paradigm case of Hector and Andromache. The Romans developed praise of marriage into a fine art, their love of the lapidary biographical summary encouraging them to take a rounded view of a partnership, of what it had achieved and how it had fared over the years. They certainly believed that some marriages were happy, characterized by co-operation, by each party knowing what the other required, even by a degree of shared interests. We have many Latin tombstones which relate in poetic terms and forms how a marriage was blessed in this way, usually placing the credit at the door of the wife. However, they rarely if ever make any mention of love. For the Roman upper classes of the first centuries BC and AD (the classes for and by whom the poetry of the period was written), marriage was usually arranged and the parties were frequently of vastly different ages. If emotional intimacy failed to develop it was scarcely surprising, and it does not surprise in turn that the love poetry of the age makes little mention of marriage, dealing instead with stolen trysts, adulterous affairs, and the ups and downs of sleeping around.

Outside formal upper-class marriage, however, lifelong, loving unions might develop. Slaves working in the same household were generally free to form partnerships, and they might well be freed together by an indulgent master and become man and wife in the eyes of the law. Masters might fall for their own female slaves and free them to take them as their own wives; such relationships were not necessarily more exploitative than other marriages, and many were clearly deeply loving. Marriage for love or sexual attraction becomes more visible in the second and third centuries AD, and tombstones set up to women by men start to praise more than just their economic, 'wifely' virtues. Such matters were never entirely forgotten, however, even in the most irregular circumstances. A charming verse inscription to Allia Potestas, a freed-woman who seems to have lived with two young lovers and possibly one older one as well, praises her both for her gorgeous, sexy figure, and for being immensely practical and efficient. Unfortunately we can only offer you a brief extract of this remarkable memorial (*see* p. 52).

The concept, the ideal of wedded love had always existed. In the throes of her passion, Catullus' Lesbia declared her readiness to marry him – thus provoking his sceptical comment on what women say in such situations (*see* p. 78). And Horace's Lydia draws a neat distinction between torrid, ephemeral love and the deeper, stronger, longer-lasting sort that makes you want to spend your life with someone else and die, not for them, but *with* them (*see* p. 60). It took a while for the sequel to these themes to be explored, but by the time of Ausonius, in the fourth century AD, it was possible to sing a song of praise to the elderly couple whose love is as fresh as the day it was born, and who therefore remain truly young at heart (*see* p. 14).

What, finally, of our translations? What, indeed, of the translation into modern English of Classical poetry in general? 'There is a sort of Books now a days,' wrote a disgruntled reader in a letter to the press in 1730, 'that I can't account for, nor see the use of them. I mean *Translations of Greek and Latin Poets into English Prose.*' Another correspondent used a striking metaphor to describe the phenomenon: it was like making the ancient poets get down from Pegasus, the winged horse of mythology, and walk on foot. But he pointed out the greater evil: translation into *bad* English verse. 'And yet I don't know whether they have not equipped them still worse who, instead of Pegasus, have mounted them upon an ambling Ass, as so many of our modern versifiers have done.'

The two modern versifiers responsible for this book would be delighted if they had succeeded in deploying anything even remotely equine to convey the invalid forms of their translations. By and large they have cheerfully taken advantage of the modern ambiguity over what poetry actually is, to leave it unclear whether they were attempting to write it. Like many educated in Britain since the 1960s, they received little instruction in the distinguishing features of poetry and were left to conclude that the main one was its curious typographical layout. This is to alert you, should you have to read it out, to do so in a slightly sing-song voice. Notions of 'the poetic' as a concrete quality are hopelessly out of date. The result is that those who discern the superficiality of layout and tone of voice can be forgiven for concluding that poetry doesn't exist.

In fact, not only does poetry exist, it also differs considerably from even the most imaginative and stirring prose, in a way which no typesetter could hope to convey. It often needs to be liberated from the domain of type, the printed page, for this to be apparent. Learned by heart and recited aloud, poetry is a different beast altogether. This is especially true of Greek and Latin verse, whose complex, rhythmical numbers and chopping-changing musical beat made it immediately identifiable to its audience. Furthermore, ancient poetry, like its modern counterpart, also relied on the apposite image, the careful choice of vocabulary, and the tools of understatement and heavy emphasis, to activate in the hearer the sentiment intended by the poet.

These two qualities, one of form and one of character, are enough to defeat most translators. Ancient rhythms have no equivalent in modern English verse, though Milton and others tried to rectify this. Scanning, rhyming lines are the traditional option for ordinary mortals, and when feeling brave we have attempted this. As for the original poetic element in each specific text selected, well, this has always been hard to get across. Our efforts will merely show the truth of Robert Frost's observation: 'Poetry is what is lost in translation'.

So what we offer is merely a collection of oddly worded cribs, whereby to understand the well-known Greek and Latin originals. You should be able to get the gist of each poem from our translation. But if you want to know what the originals are really like, we implore you: let our menagerie of asses and broken-winded old nags amble off into the distance, learn Latin and Greek, and read the ancient texts directly.

Uxor vivemus ut viximus et teneamus
  nomina quae primo sumpsimus in thalamo.

Wife, let us live as we have lived, and keep
Those names we took when first in bed together.
Nor let any day see change wrought in us by age,
When I cease to be your lad, and you my lass.
Though I am more advanced in age than Nestor,
And you rival and outdo Deiphobe of Cumae,
Let's stay unaware of what ripe old age might be;
The passing years are to be valued, not totted up.

AUSONIUS, *Epigrams* 20

Painted roundel (from a wall painting) with portraits of a man and
a woman. Roman, from Pompeii, Italy, c.30 BC–AD 50. Diam. 14 cm.
British Museum 1856,1226.1621, bequeathed by Sir William Temple.

Δάκρυά μοι σπένδουσαν ἐπήρατον οἰκτρὰ Θεανω
εἶχον ὑπὲρ λέκτρων πάννυχον ἡμετέρων.

All night Theano does nothing but cry to me in bed!
When the Evening Star falls towards Olympus,
She starts to curse the approaching dawn.
Mortals are so hard to please! If you really want to be
A slave to love, you'll need long, northern nights.

PAUL THE SILENTIARY, *Anthologia Palatina* v 283

Isaac Oliver (1556–1617), *Antiope*. Black chalk drawing.
English. 19.4 x 27.9 cm. British Museum 1869,0612.295.

Ubi amans complexust amantem,
ubi ad labra labella adiungit.

It's lover holding lover,
It's mouth to mouth;
It's a close-quarter bout between lad and wench,
And the kissing's well and truly French.
Chest to breast is pressed,
Or, in other words, it's one on one.

Then the sweetest gesture:
My pale-handed darling
Offers me her loving cup.
There's no angst or tension,
Not a single hurtful word;
Perfumes, ointments, crowns with laurels
Richly fixed, are proffered.

Keep it coming,
    Bring on more:
But ask nought of me
    When I'm done for.

PLAUTUS, *Pseudolus* 1259–68

The Great Dish from the Mildenhall treasure.
Silver, Roman Britain, fourth century AD. Found in Mildenhall,
Suffolk. Diam. 60.5 cm. British Museum 1946,1007.1.

Στέφος πλέκων ποτ᾽ εὗρον
ἐν τοῖς ῥόδοις Ἔρωτα.

Plaiting a garland one day
I came upon Love among the roses.
By the wings I caught him,
In my wine I dunked him,
And gulped him down.
And now, deep within,
His feathers tickle my insides.

Anacreontea 6

Wall painting showing wine, women and dance at a
festival. From a tomb at the Villa Pamphili, Rome,
c. AD 50. 21.5 x 65 cm. British Museum 1873,0208.1.

Liber eram, et vacuo meditabar vivere lecto.

I was free, and had no mind to share my bed;
But peace broke out and I was snared by Love.
Why should her mortal face frequent this earth?
Jupiter, your ancient transgressions are forgiven!
Her hair is auburn, her hands are long, her stature
Tall; she bears it worthily of Jupiter's own sister,
Or like Athena, striding to the Ithacan altars,
Shielding her breast with the Gorgon's serpent locks.
She's like Ischomache, the Lapiths' heroic child,
Ravished greedily amid the wine by Centaurs;
Or like Brimo, who, its said, on a Thessalian shore,
Stretched out her virgin form by Mercury.
Give up, you goddesses whom once the shepherd saw
Disrobing on the mountain side of Ida.
Would that age refrain from altering this beauty,
Though she live as long as the Cumaean prophetess.

PROPERTIUS ii 2

Andrea Verrocchio, *Head of a Woman*. Charcoal drawing. Italian,
c. AD 1475. 32.5 x 27.2 cm. British Museum 1895,0915.785.

Ἀ φιλέρως χαροποῖς Ἀσκληπιὰς οἷα γαλήνης
ὄμμασι συμπείθει πάντας ἐρωτοπλοεῖν.

Asclepias loves to love. With looks that please
She charms all comers to sail on her love's tranquil seas.

MELEAGER, *Anthologia Palatina* v 256

Marble statue of a naked Aphrodite crouching at her bath.
Roman, second century AD. H. 120 cm. British Museum
1963,1029.1, on permanent loan from the Royal Collection.

Interea magno misceri murmure caelum
incipit; insequitur commixta grandine nimbus.

The sky begins to churn and rumble deeply;
The downpour starts, with bursts of hail.
In desperate flight across the fields all turn and run,
The scattered cover seeking; the Trojan youth, their Tyrian friends,
Aphrodite's grandson. Cascading water streaks the hillsides.
One cave receives both Dido, leading, and the Trojan leader.
Ancient Mother Earth and Juno, the wedding sponsor, give a sign:
Lightning fizzes through the air in witness of the marriage.
On mountain tops the nymphs are heard to howl.

That day began the tale of Dido's death, the tale of woe.
For appearance or repute she spares no thought;
Her mind is not to carry on a secret love affair.
Marriage is the name she shrouds her guilt beneath.

VIRGIL, *Aeneid* iv 160–72

J. M. W. Turner, *Weathercote Cave, near Ingleton, when half-filled with Water and the Entrance Impassable*. Watercolour. English, c. AD 1818. 29.9 x 42.1 cm. British Museum 1910,0212.281, bequeathed by George Salting.

τὸ στόμα ταῖς χαρίτεσσι, προσώπατα δ᾽ ἄνθεσι βάλλει,
ὄμματα τῆι Παφίηι, τὼ χέρε τῆι κιθάρηι.

From your lips darts loveliness, flowers from your face,
Love fires from both your eyes, your hands shoot music's grace.
With your looks you rob their sight, their ears you stop with song.
Poor men! Pursued from every side, the hunt will not last long.

MACEDONIUS, *Anthologia Palatina* v 231

Mummy portrait of a woman in encaustic on limewood.
From Hawara, Egypt. Roman period, AD 55–70.
35.8 x 20.2 cm. British Museum EA 74716.

Cras amet qui numquam amavit quique amavit cras amet.

Tomorrow there'll be love for who has never loved,
Tomorrow there'll be love for who has loved.

Spring, the world's true birth, is here, song-singing spring;
True pacts are made of love, true weddings on the wing;
'Mid fertile showers the woodland lets her locks flow free.
Tomorrow, in the forest shade, she that binds in pairs
Will enfold the leafy dwellings in her laurel snares;
Enthroned on high, Dione will her law decree.

Tomorrow there'll be love for who has never loved,
Tomorrow there'll be love for who has loved.

To the myrtle grove the goddess bids the nymphs resort;
With the lasses goes the lad. Who would have thought
Love was on holiday, had be brought his darts today?
'Go, my nymphs, he's put his weapons down; Love's at rest.
His orders are to go unarmed; today his order is, undressed,
To hurt no living thing, with bow nor dart nor flame.
But still take care, my nymphs, Cupid's beauty stays the same.
Even when unclothed, Love is armed cap-à-pié.'

Tomorrow there'll be love for who has never loved,
Tomorrow there'll be love for who has loved!

Anon., first or second century AD: *Pervigilium Veneris* 1–8, 28–35

Francesco Xanto Avelli da Rovigo (attrib.), front of plate from a birth set,
Venus and Cupids in Vulcan's Forge. Maiolica. From Urbino, Italy, AD 1539. Diam.
17.1 cm. British Museum 1878,1230.373, bequeathed by John Henderson.

φέρ᾽ ὕδωρ, φέρ᾽ οἶνον, ὦ παῖ, φέρε δ᾽ἀνθεμόεντας ἡμῖν
στεφάνους ἔνεικον, ὡς δὴ πρὸς Ἔρωτα πυκταλίζω.

Bring water, bring wine, boy, and bring us
Wreaths of flowers. I mean to box with Love.

ANACREON. fr. 396

Bronze figurine of a reclining banqueter. Said to be from the Sanctuary
of Zeus at Dodona. Greek, sixth century BC. H. 10.2 cm. British Museum
1954,1018.1, purchased with contribution from The Art Fund.

Asper eram, et bene discidium me ferre loquebar.

I was bitter, and said being apart was 'not a problem'.
But now, that lofty fortitude has quite deserted me.
Instead, I'm like a spinning top, lashed over level ground
By the practised skill of an agile boy.
I've been a beast: brand me; rack me (maybe then
I'll keep my little pomposities to myself); rein in
My graceless comments. Spare me, however;
I beg you by the pacts of our stolen love,
By Venus, and by our consummated passion.

TIBULLUS i 5, 1–8

Panel from a mosaic showing a lion and cupids. From Naples, Italy.
Roman, c.70–10 BC. 37.2 x 37.7 cm. British Museum 1856,1213.5.

Μεσονυκτίοις ποτ᾽ ὥραις
στρεφέτην ὅτ᾽ Ἄρκτος ἤδη
κατὰ χεῖρα τὴν Βοώτου.

Once, deep in the night
When the Bear has turned
By the hand of the Herdsman,
And all mortal men
Lie spent from toil,
Came a knock at my door.
And there stood – Cupid.
'Who's that beating my door down,
Tearing my dreams to shreds'
'Open up,' said Cupid,
'I'm just a toddler, no need to fret.
I'm soaked through, and a bit lost
On this moonless night.'
Well, I felt sorry at his tale,
Quickly lit my lamp,
Opened up, to see this child –
With bow, quiver, and wings.
He sat by the fire.

I warmed his hands in mine,
From his hair
I squeezed the damp.
When the cold had gone, he
Said, 'Let's try my bow, maybe
The wet has spoiled the string.
And he drew, and he hit me
Full in the chest – and it stung!
Up he jumped with a giggle.
'My friend,' he said, 'Great news!
My bow may not be broken.
But soon your heart will be.'

Anacreontea 33

William Wynne Ryland, *Dormio Innocuus*. Engraving
after a painting by Angelica Kauffman. English, AD 1776.
36 x 31 cm. British Museum 1860,1110.25.

DORMIO INNOCUUS: VIX IMPUNE EXPERGEFECERIS.

From an Original Picture in the Collection of His Grace the Duke of Northumberland,
to whom this Plate is humbly Inscribed by His Graces most obliged & obedient Servant, Wᵐ Wynne Ryland.

Published May 21ˢᵗ 1776 by the Proprietor Nᵒ 159, near Somerset House in the Strand.

Ποικιλόθρον᾽ ἀθανάτ᾽ Ἀφροδιτα,
παῖ Δίος δολόπλοκε, λίσσομαί σε.

Aphrodite divine, enthroned in splendour,
Beguiling daughter of Zeus, I beg you,
My lady, slay not my spirit
With pain and grief.   .

But come to me now, if ever
My distant cries you once heard
And came, leaving your father's
Hall, golden

Chariot yoked, while pretty sparrows
Brought you quickly over black earth,
Fluttering wings from heaven
Through the air, and

Quickly they appeared. Blessed one,
Your immortal face smiled,
You asked what was wrong this time,
Why I called you,

What my mad heart pined for most.
'Who is it now that needs charming
Back to your love; Sappho,
Who does you wrong?

'For she may run now, but soon she'll be
    after you.
If she takes no gifts, yet she will give.
And if now she loves you not, either way,
She will.'

Come to me even now, from sagging
Infatuation deliver me; fulfil all my spirit's
Longings. Come,
Be my comrade.

SAPPHO. fr. 1

Ἔρως ἀντίκατε μάχαν,
Ἔρως, ὃς ἐν κτήμασι πίπτεις.

Love, unbeaten in battle,
Love, plunderer of wealth,
You keep your night-watch on
The soft cheeks of a girl,
Roaming across oceans,
At home in the wilderness.
None of the deathless ones
Escapes you, nor any who
Live for a day.
To possess you is to lose all mind.

Even good souls
To shame and ruin you drag askew.
Family you have set at odds,
Blood versus blood.
Desire swelling from the eyes
Of the lovely bride wins out,
Enthroned in might and as
Powerful as strong law.
Untouchable, she plays with us,
Divine Aphrodite.

SOPHOCLES, *Antigone* 781–801

William Blake, *The Judgment of Paris*. Watercolour. English, AD 1811.
38.5 x 46 cm. British Museum 1949,1112.4, donated by W. Graham Robertson.

Ματρὸς ἔτ᾽ ἐν κόλποισιν ὁ νήπιος ὀρθρινὰ παίζων
ἀστραγάλους τοὐμὸν πνεῦμ᾽ ἐκύβευσεν Ἔρως.

On his mother's lap young Cupid is at play,
For my heart his dice he casts each day.

MELEAGER, *Anthologia Palatina* xii 47

Silver medallion with Aphrodite seated on a rock. From Taranto,
southern Italy, c.300–200 BC. Diam. 9.3 cm. British Museum 1853,0314.1.

43

Siqua ricordanti benefacta priora voluptas
   est homini.

If one can garner any pleasure in reviewing one's good deeds,
   In thinking just how dutiful one's been,
How one's betrayed no solemn trust, nor in any pact or deal
   Cited gods in vain, intending to mislead,
What pleasures for your dotage, poet, you have laid in store,
   The products of this thankless love affair.
Doing right by someone else, in every word and every act;
   At every point you could do this, you have.
But it's all been thrown away, spent without return of thanks.
   What on earth's the point in dragging out the pain?
Why not take a bold decision, why not simply walk away?
   The gods don't want you wretched: why not stop?
It's hard to make a break when you've been together a long time.
   It's hard; but do it, any way you can.

CATULLUS 76

Käthe Kollwitz, *Female Nude Seen from Behind*.
Lithograph. German, AD 1903. 57.5 x 44 cm. British Museum
1951,0501.79, bequeathed by Campbell Dodgson.

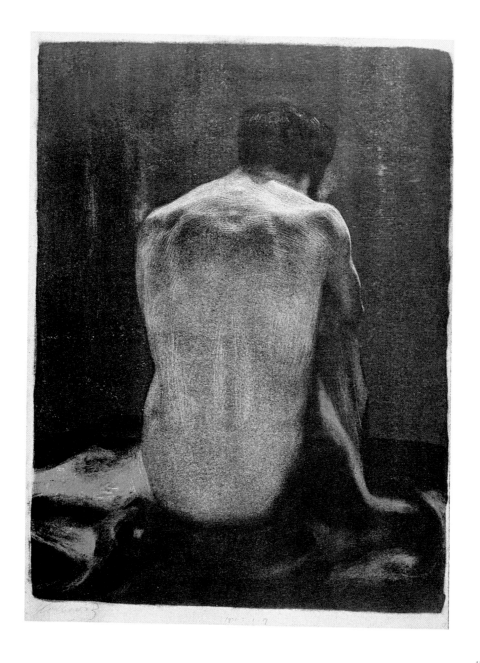

Τὴν ψυχήν, Ἀγάθωνα φιλῶν, ἐπὶ χείλεσιν ἔσχον.
ἦλθε γὰρ ἡ τλήμων ὡς διαβησομένη.

Kissing Agathon, I held my life on my lips.
It wanted to pass over, poor thing, into him.

'PLATO'. *Anthologia Palatina* v 78

Ἀστὴρ πρὶν μὲν ἔλαμπες ἐνὶ ζωοῖσιν Ἐῶιος.
νῦν δὲ θανὼν λάμπεις Ἕσπερος ἐν φθιμένοις.

Once among the living you shone like the morning star.
Now gone, your evening star shines among the dead.

'PLATO', *Anthologia Palatina* vii 670

Detail of a pavement from St-Romain-en-Gal, Vienne, France. Second half
of second century AD. 2.74 x 2.74 m. British Museum 1913,1013.1.

Odi et amo. Quare id faciam, fortasse requiris?
  Nescio, sed fieri sentio et excrucior.

I hate and I love. Why should I do that, perhaps you ask?
I've no idea; but I feel it happen, and it tortures me.

CATULLUS 85

Black-glazed drinking vessel with seated hunter. Pottery, Etruscan, c.300–280 BC.
Diam. 17.8 cm. British Museum 1855,0306.16, donated by Chambers Hall.

Ὄμματ᾽ ἔχεις Ἥρης, Μελίτη, τας χεῖρας Ἀθήνης,
τοὺς μάζους Παφίης, τὰ σφυρὰ τῆς Θέτιδος.

You have the eyes of Hera, Athena's hands,
Aphrodite's tender breasts, Thetis' slender ankles.
Happy he who but looks, thrice-blest who hears your voice,
Near-divine who kisses, all god who has you for his own.

RUFINUS, *Anthologia Palatina* v 94

Pierre-Paul Prud'hon, *Standing Female Nude*. Black chalk drawing.
French, c. AD 1810. 62.5 x 41.5 cm. British Museum 1968,0210.18,
bequeathed by César Mange de Hauke.

Haec sibi non placuit, numquam sibi libera visa.

She was not self-satisfied; she never considered herself
Free of obligations.
Her eyes shone bright, her beautiful hair glistened gold,
Her face never lost that ivory glow
Which no mortal woman is supposed to have had,
And the nipples were pert on her snow-white breast.
And as for her legs – well,
She had the very stance of Atalanta on the comic stage.
She didn't starve herself, but bore her curvaceous form
With grace. She hunted after every hair on her body.
That her hands were hard might be a reproach
(Nothing met her standards unless she did it herself).

Inscription from Rome, second century AD: *CIL* vi 37965

Marble bust of 'Clytie'. Said to be from near Naples, Italy.
Roman, c. AD 40–50. H. 57.2 cm. British Museum 1805,0703.79.

Quaeris, quot mihi basiationes
Tuae, Lesbia, satis sint superque?

You ask, Lesbia, how many kisses I find
Enough for me, and how many too many.

As many as are the grains of laserine sands
Of Libya, lying in Cyrene's lands,
By the oracle, to Jove the fervid founded,
And the tomb of long-gone Battus bounded;
Or as many as are the stars, within whose sight,
Men's secret loves take place in silent night.

Thus often you may bestow your osculations,
Enough and more Catullus' esurience;
Measureless to the curious' calculations,
And warding off wicked tongues' bedevilments.

CATULLUS 7

Aeneadum genetrix, hominum divumque voluptas, alma Venus.

Mother of the house of Aeneas, delight of gods and men,
Cherishing Venus, by whom the ship-crossed sea,
By whom the fruitful lands beneath the wandering stars
Are filled with life, through thee each and every race
Of living thing is brought to be, is in sunlight raised.
Thee, Goddess, the winds flee, the clouds in the sky
Fly before thee and thy coming, for thee manifold Earth
Puts out a sweet carpet of flowers, the broad expanse of ocean
Smiles, and the serene sky glows with shimmering light.

LUCRETIUS, *De Rerum Natura* i 1–9

Lucas Cranach, the Elder, *Venus and Cupid*.
Chiaroscuro woodcut. German, AD 1508. 27.6 x 18.7 cm.
British Museum 1895,0122.268, donated by William Mitchell.

Ἔρος δηὖτέ μ᾿ ὁ λυσιμέλης δόνει,
  γλυκύπικρον ἀμάχανον ὄρπετον.

Yet again I'm hamstrung by Love. He's shaken me up,
That sweet-bitter, impossible creature.

SAPPHO. fr. 130

Δέδυκε μὲν ἀ σελάννα
και Πληιάδες, μέσαι δέ
νύκτες, παρὰ δ᾽ ἔρχετ ὤρα,
ἐγὼ δὲ μόνα καθεύδω.

The moon has set,
Pleiades too. It's the middle of
The night, time passes.
But I sleep alone.

SAPPHO (?). *Poetae Melici Graeci* fr. 976

Edward Burne Jones, *Love in a Tangle*. Watercolour. English,
AD 1882–98. Diam. 16.2 cm. British Museum 1909,0512.1.15.

Donec gratus eram tibi.

While you still wanted me there,
While there was no other lad whose arms
You'd rather have around your snowy
    neck,
Then I was happier than the Persian
    Shah.

'While I still scorched you most of all,
While Lydia had yet to yield to Chloe,
Then I, Lydia (of wide renown), had
Greater glory than the mother of the
    Roman twins.'

I do homage now to Thracian Chloe;
Sweetly she sings, expertly she plays the
    lyre.
For Chloe I shall never shrink from
    death,
If my sweetheart's life is saved.

'I now share a burning passion,
With Calaïs, Ornytus's son from
    Thurium.
For him I'll suffer death twice over,
If my dear boy's life is saved.'

What if our love of old returns,
And yokes us back together with a beam
    of bronze?
What if blonde Chloe is ushered out,
And cast-off Lydia finds the door wide
    open?

'He may be more handsome than a star;
And you more fickle than a cork,
More stormy than the cruel Adriatic; but
With you I'd love to live, with you I'd
    gladly die.'

HORACE iii 9

Detail from The Portland Vase. Cameo glass. Perhaps from Rome, Italy, c. AD 5–25. H. 24 cm. British Museum 1945,0927.1, purchased with the aid of a bequest from James Rose Vallentin.

Foeda est in coitu et brevis voluptas

Sex is but brief, degrading fun,
And quickly palls when it is done.
So let's not, like livestock filled with carnal greed,
Rush blind and headlong at the deed;
Such love goes stale, the flame is burned.
But thus, with business evermore adjourned,
Let's lie together and just kiss.
There's no toil, no cause for shame in this.
It pleased, it pleases, it long will please;
It ever starts and knows no cease.

PETRONIUS 28

Red-figured cup attributed to the Brygos Painter showing a
symposium scene (detail of the inside). Greek, c.490–480 BC.
H. 12.7 cm. British Museum 1848,0619.7.

Σφαίρηι δηὖτέ με πορφυρῆι
βάλλων χρυσοκόμης Ἔρως.

Love, golden-haired boy, tosses
His purple ball to me one more time,
Invites me to play
With the girl in colourful sandals.

But she's from towering Lesbos,
And my hair, being white,
She despises. She's gasping
For another girl . . .

ANACREON. fr. 358

Porcelain group of Pygmalion and Galatea.
From Sèvres, France, c. AD 1764–73. H. 36.1 cm.
British Museum 1948,1203.38, Sir Bernard Eckstein.

Aestus erat, mediamque dies exegerat horam.

A sweltering summer's day; afternoon wore on.
I took my place in the middle of the couch.
The shutters on the window were half open, half closed,
Giving that light you get in woodland,
Like the half-light of dusk, after sunset,
Or when night has gone, day not yet arrived.
It's the light that timid girls like;
a light to cloak their shyness in.
And here's Corinna, draped in a short tunic,
Her parted hair flowing down her snowy neck.

I tugged at her dress. Skimpy as it was,
It didn't hide much, though still she fought to keep it on.
But the fight was one she wanted to lose –
Happily defeated, she gave herself up.

Those shoulders; those arms . . . I looked, I stroked . . .
Those nipples prompt, inviting;
Those tumescent breasts above a slimline stomach;
Those long, fine curves, those girlish thighs . . .
No more specifics. What I saw was faultless.
I held her naked body, tight to mine.
As for what followed, you'll guess. Tired out, we slept.
More afternoons like this? I'd not say no.

OVID, *Amores* i 5

William Bell Scott, *Interior with a Man and a Woman embracing on a Sofa*.
Brush drawing. English, AD 1863. 12.5 x 17.3 cm. British Museum 1974,0615.7.

Inventa nuper, nervum cum tenderet acrem,
  obstupuit visa victus Amor dominam.

Scarce had he spied her when, drawing tight his bowstring,
  Love stared dumbfounded at the vision of my lady.
Delighting in her power, as she ran off, she cast a backward
  Glance: he too has taken to his heels, swifter than the wind.
But, as he runs, by chance his quivers full have fallen,
  Which she retrieves, spoils of the conquered god,
And hoists up on her shoulder. Now men and gods alike
  By her alone are smitten. Love strays, defeated and disarmed.

MARULLUS, *Epigrams* i 3

Guglielmo Morghen, *Venus Disarming Cupid*. Engraving. Italian,
late AD 1780s. 42.3 x 30 cm (image). British Museum 1837,0408.369.

Hospes, quod deico paullum est: asta ac pellege

Passer-by, I've not much to say: stop and read it through.
This is the unlovely tomb of a lovely woman.
Her parents called her Claudia by name.
Her husband she loved with all her heart.
Two sons she bore; one she leaves behind her
On earth, the other she placed beneath it.
Her conversation was elegant, but her bearing proper.
She kept house, she span her wool. That's all. Go your way.

Inscription from Rome, first century BC: *CIL* i² 1266

Limestone head of a woman. Roman, c.50–30 BC.
H. 28 cm. British Museum 1879,0712.15.

Invisus natalis adest, qui rure molesto
  et sine Cerintho tristis agendus erit.

The loathsome birthday's come; it's to be glumly passed
In rural boredom, with Cerinthus nowhere near.
What is sweeter than the city? Is a girl to be content
With a country cabin by some chilly Tuscan brook?
Be still, dear guardian, you do too much for me;
Trips away from home are often far from timely.
You may remove me but my heart and soul will stay,
Even though I'm not allowed to act as I would wish.

Scis iter ex animo sublatum triste puellae?
  natali Romae iam licet esse suo.

That dreary trip's no longer on your girlfriend's mind;
She's now allowed to spend the day in Rome!
So let us all celebrate my birthday now –
Since now perhaps it's what you least expected.

SULPICIA iii 14, a and b

John Robert Cozens, *Lake Nemi*. Watercolour. Italian,
AD 1777–8. 36 x 52.2 cm. British Museum 1958,0712.332,
bequeathed by Robert Wylie Lloyd.

Tu mihi, tu certe, memini, Graecine negabas,
uno posse aliquem tempore amare duas.

You it was, Graecinus, yes, you that said
'No man can love two girls at once'. I was misled.
I dropped my guard, and now, in love-rat fashion,
I give two girls at once my undivided passion.

They're both real belles, both well turned out,
Which is the more accomplished is in doubt.
Number one is prettier – and so is number two;
Which gives me greater pleasure? Both of 'em do!

OVID, *Amores* ii 10, 1–8

Mariano Bovi, *Emma, Lady Hamilton, Dancing the Tarantalla*. Coloured
engraving. English, AD 1796. 38.5 x 29.7 cm. British Museum 1906,0719.5.

Drawn by Wm Locke Esq.   London Published by Mrs Bew, 3 St James Picadilly, May 15 1798.   Engraved by Mr Bovi

φαίνεταί μοι κῆνος ἴσος θέοισιν
ἔμμεν' ὤνηρ, ὄττις ἐνάντιός τοι
ἰσδάνει.

Supremely blest, like a god, he seems to me,
That man who sits across from you,
And, moving close, gives in to your
Darling voice,

Your delightful laugh – I swear, it
Makes my heart thump within my chest.
When I catch just a glimpse of you,
Words won't come,

My tongue freezes, a subtle
Fire snakes beneath my skin,
There's no sight in my eyes, my ears
Pound,

Sweat pours down, a shiver takes me
Entire, I'm paler than grass.
Not much more of this, I know,
And I'll die.

SAPPHO, fr. 31

Marble head of woman. From the Temple of Artemis at Ephesos.
Greek, c. 550–520 BC. H. 19 cm. British Museum 1873,0505.43.

Nulli se dicit mulier mea nubere malle
    quam mihi, non si se Iuppiter ipse petat.
dicit: sed mulier cupido quod dicit amanti,
    in vento et rapida scribere oportet aqua.

There's none she'd rather wed, my woman says,
Than me – not if Jupiter himself should woo her.
Aye, so she says.

But what a woman says to her overheated lover . . .
Well, you can write it on the wind,
And in swiftly-flowing water.

CATULLUS 70

Dante Gabriel Rossetti, *Writing on the Sand*. Watercolour. English,
AD 1859. 26.3 x 24.1 cm. British Museum 1886,0607.14.

χρῆν μὲν κατὰ καιρὸν ἐρώ–
    των δρέπεσθαι, θυμέ, σὺν ἁλικίαι.

My heart, you should have harvested your longings
At the right time – in your youth.
But anyone who's seen the sunlight
Shimmering from Theoxenus' eyes,
And is not thrown on waves of desire
Has a black heart, forged of iron or steel

In a cold fire (disdained by Aphrodite's quick glance
He breaks his back for money, or
Persists like a foolish female on
His path, however cold).
But when I look on this boy's fresh-limbed youth,

Stung by fire at Her divine whim
I melt like holy beeswax.
For Attraction is at home on Tenedos' isle,
And Charm raised Agesilas' son.

PINDAR, fr. 123

The Strangford Apollo. Said to be from the island of Anáfi, Cyclades.
Greek, c. 500–490 BC. 1.01 m. British Museum 1864,0220.1.

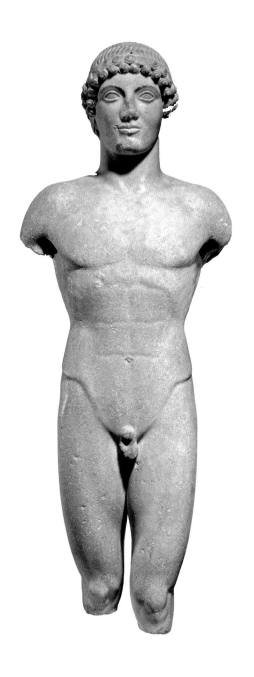

Ἁ μεγάλα μοὶ Κύπρις ἔθ᾽ ὑπνόωντι παρέστα,
νηπίαχον τὸν Ἔρωτα καλᾶς ἐκ χειρὸς ἄγοισα.

Great Aphrodite came to me once in my sleep
Leading little Eros by the hand – he
Stared shyly at the ground. She spoke,
'Dear rustic swain, take this lad, and teach him to sing.'
She goes, and I, fool, teach Love my songs,
How Pan invented pipes, Athena the flute,
Hermes the lyre, sweet Apollo the harp.
So I taught him, but he pays no heed.
He sings his own songs, of the loves
Of gods and men, his mother's works.
What I taught him then I now clean forget,
But what he taught me stays with me yet.

BION. 5

Edward Burne Jones, *Cupid finding Psyche*. Watercolour. English, AD1866.
66.8 x 47.6 cm. British Museum 1954,0508.8, bequeathed by Cecil French.

Ἔρως Ἔρως, ὁ κατ᾽ ὀμμάτων
στάζεις πόθον, εἰσάγων γλυκεῖαν
ψυχᾶι χάριν οὓς ἐπιστρατεύσηι.

Love, O Love, dripping liquid desire
Down upon the eyes, inducing
Sweet pleasure in the objects of your war,
I pray you never come to me
To harm or disconcert.
For no shaft of fire or star
Is like that thrown from
The hand of Love, Zeus' son.

It's all in vain that Greece should
Slaughter its cattle by Alpheus
In Delphi's precincts.
For we dishonour Love,
Mankind's despot,
Who holds the key to Aphrodite's
Conclaves of delight.
For he, when he comes, brings only ruin,
And every species of calamity to man.

EURIPIDES, *Hippolytus* 525–41

Bronze statuette of Venus or her mother Dione. Roman, probably second century AD.
H. 30. 5 cm. British Museum 1824,0428.1, bequeathed by Richard Payne Knight.

Ἔρος αὖτέ με κυανέοισιν ὑπὸ
βλεφάροις τακέρ᾽ ὄμμασι δερκόμενος.

Once again Love gazes at me from under his dark lashes,
melting me with his eyes.
With his assorted lures
He coaxes me into Aphrodite's endless snares.

How I shudder at his coming –
Like an old champion team-horse, forced
Under the chariot-yoke and back into the race.

IBYCUS, fr. 287

Mummy portrait of Artemidorus. From Hawara, Egypt. Roman period, c. AD 100–120.
L. 1.71 m. British Museum 1888,0806.8, donated by Henry Martyn Kennard.

ὡς εἰπὼν οὗ παιδὸς ὀρέξατο φαίδιμος Ἕκτωρ.
ἂψ δ' ὁ πάϊς πρὸς κόλπον ἐϋζώνοιο τιθήνης
ἐκλίνθη ἰάχων.

Thus spoke glorious Hector, and he reached out for his son.
But the child screamed, and shrank back into the bosom
Of his nurse, frightened at his father's appearance,
Terrified at the bronze and the horse-haired crest
Nodding threateningly from the top of his helmet.
His father and his lady mother laughed out loud.
And glorious Hector took his helmet from his head
And laid it, flashing brightly, on the ground.
Then he kissed his dear son and swung him in his arms . . .
He put the child back into the arms of his mother.
She took him into her fragrant bosom
Smiling in her tears. This her husband noticed, and he felt for her.
He stroked her with his hand, and spoke to her,
'My lady, do not break your heart with grief for me.
No man will send me to Hades before my time . . .'
Thus spoke glorious Hector, and he took up his horse-plumed
Helmet, and his wife went away homewards.
But she kept on looking back, and she cried a flood of tears.

HOMER, *Iliad* vi, 482–96

Red-figured amphora attributed to the Libation Painter showing
a warrior departing. Greek, c.350–325 BC. H. 53.7 cm. British Museum
1856,1226.12, bequeathed by Sir William Temple.

BIOGRAPHICAL NOTES

ANACREON (mid to late sixth century BC): a Greek writer of mostly love poems and drinking songs whose style was much imitated later by the anonymous authors of the *Anacreontea*.

AUSONIUS (died *c.* AD 395): statesman and man of letters, from Burdigala (Bordeaux) in Roman Gaul. He was a Christian, but his numerous poems deal with Classical themes, often in novel, slightly self-conscious ways, and frequently reflect a deep familiarity with Virgil.

BION (late second century BC): known mostly as a Greek writer of pastoral, or bucolic, poetry.

CATULLUS (*c.*84–*c.*54 BC): born into a wealthy provincial family at Verona, he left 116 poems, mostly short, often deliberately reminiscent of Greek verse of the Hellenistic age. Many deal with aspects of his long affair with the aristocratic Clodia, whom he referred to as 'Lesbia'.

EURIPIDES (*c.*480–406 BC): together with Aeschylus and Sophocles, one of the three Athenian tragedians. Nineteen of his ninety-two plays survive.

HOMER (eighth century BC): the name given in antiquity to the putative author of the two great epic poems the *Iliad* and the *Odyssey* usually dated to the eighth century BC. Whether the poems were made by one Homer or a Homeric tradition of many poets is a long-disputed question.

HORACE (65–8 BC): despite relatively humble birth in central Italy and serving on the wrong side in Rome's Civil Wars, Horace became one of the great poets of the Augustan regime, and a close friend of the emperor's right-hand man Maecenas. His surviving works are the *Odes*, the *Epodes*, the *Epistles*, and a verse essay on the art of poetry.

IBYCUS (mid sixth century BC): Greek lyric poet whose work survives only in fragments.

LUCRETIUS (died 55 BC): author of the *De Rerum Natura* (*On the Nature of*

Things), a remarkable epic poem in six books presenting Epicurean natural philosophy. Saint Jerome reported that it was composed in the intervals between fits of madness brought on by a love-philtre. Book IV of the work fiercely condemns passionate love.

MACEDONIUS (mid sixth century AD): poet and consul, a senior official, in the reign of the Byzantine Emperor Justinian (reigned AD 527–65). About forty epigrams by him survive in the Greek Anthology.

MICHAEL MARULLUS (AD 1453–1500): classicizing poet of the Renaissance. Born to a noble Greek family in Constantinople, raised in Ragusa (Dubrovnik), he made his home in Italy where he fought as a mercenary. His verse was widely read and earned the praise of Leonardo da Vinci.

MELEAGER (mid second century to early first century BC): writer of Greek epigrams. Compiler of the *Garland*, a collection of 4,000 epigrams, including about 100 of his own.

OVID (43 BC–AD 17): a well-born central Italian, Ovid abandoned a career of public office in favour of poetry. In AD 8 he was banished from Rome, for reasons that have never been entirely clear, and he died in exile on the coast of the Black Sea. His verse ranges from love poems and a long work on the art of love to epic works on the religious calendar (the *Fasti*) and favourite mythical tales (the *Metamorphoses*).

PAUL THE SILENTIARY (mid sixth century AD): senior Byzantine official and poet. About eighty epigrams of his survive, together with a verse description of the Church of the Holy Wisdom in Constantinople.

PETRONIUS (first century AD): author of the well-known *Satyricon*, he is sometimes identified with the 'arbiter of elegance' at the court of Nero. A large collection of short poems, ranging from the romantic to the scabrous, is ascribed to his name.

PINDAR (c.518–438 BC): famous for his sublime and complex poems in praise of prize-winning athletes, far more of his work survives than of other early Greek lyric poets.

PLATO (c.429–327 BC): renowned Greek philosopher to whom all Western philosophy is reputedly but a footnote. The two poems printed here are uncertainly, but attractively, attributed to him.

PLAUTUS (wrote c.200–185 BC): said to be from Sarsina in northern Umbria, Italy, a writer of Latin comedies for the stage, all based closely on Greek originals, though with much original material of his own.

RUFINUS (second to fifth centuries AD – dates not known): thirty-six epigrams survive in the name of this otherwise unknown poet in the Greek, or Palatine, Anthology.

SAPPHO (late seventh to early sixth centuries BC): an aristocratic lyric poet from Mytilene on the island of Lesbos, famous for her homoerotic poems written about and for her female companions.

SOPHOCLES (c.495–406 BC): one of the three great tragic poets of fifth-century Athens. Of his 123 plays, only seven complete ones and a portion of an eighth survive.

SULPICIA (first century AD): an aristocratic woman, brought up as ward of Tibullus' and Ovid's chief patron. She left six short elegies which have come down to us by being transmitted together with the works of Tibullus.

TIBULLUS (born c.50 BC): little is known of his life. His two surviving books of *Elegies* refer to at least two mistresses and one male paramour. Ovid (who had the same aristocratic patron) regarded him with admiration and affection.

VIRGIL (70–19 BC): Of relatively humble origin from Mantua, in northern Italy, he wrote three principal works: the *Eclogues*, the *Georgics*, and the *Aeneid*, one of the most influential works of literature in world history. All his work explicitly supported, in varying degrees, the regime of Augustus, his great patron.

GLOSSARY OF MYTHICAL AND GEOGRAPHICAL NAMES

AENEAS A Trojan prince, son of VENUS. He travelled to Italy and established a line of kings that was to culminate in the foundation of Rome.

ALPHEUS River in the Peleponnese on which Olympia stands. Personified as a widely worshipped god.

APHRODITE Greek goddess of beauty, love and sex, identified by the Romans with their VENUS.

APOLLO The archer god, responsible for sickness and its cure, and – as Phoebus Apollo – identified with the sun.

ATALANTA Virginal nymph renowned for her athleticism, and often represented in Greek and Roman comic drama as a paragon of young, leggy sexuality.

ATHENA Goddess of war and learning, who sprung fully formed from the head of ZEUS, identified by the Romans with their Minerva.

BATTUS The founder and first king of the Greek colony of CYRENE in north Africa.

BRIMO A goddess of the Underworld.

CENTAURS A race of monsters, half man and half horse.

CUMAE A Greek settlement on the coast of Campania in Italy, home to the prophetess DEIPHOBE.

CUPID The Roman personification of 'desire' (*cupido*), identified with the Greek EROS and often represented as a boy or youth shooting arrows at his victims.

CYRENE The north African kingdom West of Egypt. Known to the Greeks as a great grain exporter and the home of the desert plant 'laser' or silphium.

DEIPHOBE The name given by some writers to the 'Sibyl' or prophetess of CUMAE in Italy. Like the other Sibyls of the ancient world, represented as an aged and decrepit old woman.

DELPHI A holy site in central Greece, home to the most revered oracle of APOLLO.

DIDO Queen of Carthage in north Africa. Book IV of Virgil's *Aeneid* tells of her doomed love affair with AENEAS on his way to Italy.

DIONE In early myth, the wife of ZEUS and mother by him of APHRODITE.

EROS The Greek personification of desire, identified with the Roman CUPID and often represented as a boy or youth shooting arrows at his victims.

GORGONS A group of witch-like women depicted with serpents as hair. The chief Gorgon was Medusa.

HADES King of the Underworld, and hence a name for the nether regions themselves.

HECTOR Eldest son and heir of Priam, king of Troy, killed by Achilles in the tenth year of the Trojan War.

HERA Wife of ZEUS and mother of the gods, identified by the Romans with their JUNO.

HERMES Messenger of the gods, patron of commerce and other human activities, identified by the Romans with their MERCURY.

IDA A mountain of Crete, on whose slopes the infant ZEUS was hidden.

ISOMACHE The wife of the king of the LAPITHS; their marriage feast turned into a battle with the CENTAURS, by whom she was abducted.

ITHACA The island kingdom of Odysseus, on the north-west coast of Greece.

JOVE Another form of the name JUPITER, the Roman ZEUS.

JUNO Mother of the gods, the Roman equivalent of HERA.

JUPITER Father of the gods, the Roman equivalent of ZEUS. Also called JOVE.

LAPITHS A race of giants from THESSALY, famous for their war with the CENTAURS.

LESBOS A large island in the northern Aegean Sea, said to be the birthplace of Sappho.

MERCURY Messenger of the gods, the Roman equivalent of HERMES.

NESTOR An aged, much respected warrior on the Greek side in the war against Troy.

OLYMPUS The mountain in THESSALY in northern Greece traditionally and poetically regarded as home to the gods.

PAN The goat-footed, pipe-playing god of the wilderness and mountain regions, often seen as a junior partner to APOLLO.

PLEIADES The constellation in Taurus, made up of seven stars said to be the daughters of Atlas.

TENEDOS An Aegean island not far from the coast of north-west Anatolia, in the region of Troy.

THESSALY A region of central Greece.

THETIS A nymph, mother of the warrior Achilles.

THURIUM Also called Thurii, a Greek city in southern Italy.

TYRIANS The people of Tyre on the coast of Phoenicia. The inhabitants of Carthage and their queen Dido were of Tyrian stock.

VENUS The Roman goddess of beauty, love and sex, equivalent of the Greek APHRODITE.

ZEUS Father of the gods, son of Kronos and notoriously unfaithful husband of HERA. Identified by the Romans with their JUPITER.

FURTHER READING AND WEB RESOURCES

In compiling this anthology of translations, we naturally consulted others, including:

P. Jay (ed.), *The Greek Anthology* (Penguin, 1981) – a generous selection from the famous anthology of Greek epigrams, the *Anthologia Palatina*.

A. Poole and J. Maule (eds), *The Oxford Book of Classical Verse* (Oxford University Press, 1995) – excellent anthology of translations by genuine poets.

C. A. Trypanis (ed.), *The Penguin Book of Greek Verse* (Penguin, 1971) – texts and translations of poetry in Greek from Homer to the twentieth century.

M. L. West (ed.), *Greek Lyric Poetry* (1993) – translations and comment by the foremost scholar in the field.

On Latin love elegy, *see*:

R. O. A. M. Lyne, *The Latin Love Poets from Catullus to Horace* (Oxford University Press, 1980).

For far more on Classical literature and much else besides, *see*:

S. Hornblower and T. Spawforth (eds), *The Oxford Classical Dictionary* (Oxford University Press, 3rd edn, 2003) – the ultimate reference book in English on the Classical world.

M. C. Howatson (ed.) *The Oxford Companion to Classical Literature* (Oxford University Press, 1993).

The British Museum Collection online
All of the artworks illustrated in this book are from the collection of the British Museum. To find out more about objects in the British Museum's collection visit the website: britishmuseum.org.

ILLUSTRATION CREDITS

Except for those images listed below, all photographs in this book are © The Trustees of the British Museum and courtesy of the Department of Photography and Imaging.

Page
25 Royal Collection Trust / © Her Majesty Queen Elizabeth II 2012
45 © DACS 2012